T0268245

How It Ends

How It Ends

DEBBIE PATTERSON

PLAYWRIGHTS CANADA PRESS
TORONTO

How It Ends © Copyright 2022 by Debbie Patterson
First edition: January 2023
Printed and bound in Canada by Rapido Books, Montreal

Jacket design by Kisscut Design
Jacket image © AUDSHULE / Stocksy.com

Playwrights Canada Press
202-269 Richmond St. W., Toronto, ON M5V 1X1
416.703.0013 | info@playwrightscanada.com | www.playwrightscanada.com

For professional or amateur production rights, please contact Playwrights Canada Press.

LIBRARY AND ARCHIVES CANADA CATALOGUING IN PUBLICATION
Title: How it ends / Debbie Patterson.
Names: Patterson, Debbie, 1966- author.
Description: A play.
Identifiers: Canadiana (print) 20220460493 | Canadiana (ebook) 20220460531
   | ISBN 9780369104007 (softcover) | ISBN 9780369104014 (EPUB)
   | ISBN 9780369104021 (PDF)
Classification: LCC PS8631.A8465 H69 2022 | DDC C812/.6—DC23

Playwrights Canada Press operates on land which is the ancestral home of the Anishinaabe Nations (Ojibwe / Chippewa, Odawa, Potawatomi, Algonquin, Saulteaux, Nipissing, and Mississauga), the Wendat, and the members of the Haudenosaunee Confederacy (Mohawk, Oneida, Onondaga, Cayuga, Seneca, and Tuscarora), as well as Metis and Inuit peoples. It always was and always will be Indigenous land.

We acknowledge the support of the Canada Council for the Arts, the Ontario Arts Council (OAC), Ontario Creates, and the Government of Canada for our publishing activities.

Canada Council Conseil des arts
for the Arts du Canada

ONTARIO ARTS COUNCIL
CONSEIL DES ARTS DE L'ONTARIO
an Ontario government agency
un organisme du gouvernement de l'Ontario

Canada

ONTARIO | ONTARIO
CREATES | CRÉATIF

In memory of Jim Derksen, survivor, gambler, activist, father, poet, abilities mentor, visionary, Platonic thinker.

Foreword

BY MICHAEL SOBOTA

I've known Debbie Patterson since she was a young woman growing up in Thunder Bay, Ontario. She was a sassy, classy woman earning her craft and learning the mysteries of theatre and live performances. She learned a lot.

When she moved away to Winnipeg, Manitoba, to continue her career, raise a family, and become a passionate advocate on behalf of many things, including disabled communities, I saw her less often. I experienced her less often. But my admiration for who she is and what she does grew constantly.

So when an opportunity arose to go see the premier production of *How It Ends* in Winnipeg, a couple of friends and I jumped in a car and were off to see her wizardry. I didn't readily understand how apt it was to go on a journey to experience *How It Ends*.

Most plays are about journeys of some sort. And relationships. And ask questions. The good ones, anyway. Patterson's script does all of these things, weaving metaphors and metaphysics and tricks into a story about dying. How we die. How we want to die. Her layered text references Viola Spolin's *Improvisation for the Theater* and Shakespeare's *Hamlet* and Pinter's *The Homecoming* and even Rodgers and Hammerstein's *Carousel*, among others. These are heady references. Her play starts out in a familiar place: a brother and sister are fishing on a Canadian lake. They tease each other about death, like Rosencrantz and Guildenstern, until a storm arises and changes their and our perspectives.

There is an Angel in Debbie's script that constantly challenges us, asking the hard questions, prodding us to go deeper about just what death—and near death—means. I have had many near-death experiences. I've tumbled off a wall while building a log cabin with a running chainsaw in my hand. I've fallen off a roof. I've found myself in deep water, frightened that I didn't have the strength to get back to the surface. And I've been broadsided by a car while riding my bicycle to the weekend farmers' market. That one was recent. Near death can happen at any time. As can death.

How It Ends doesn't tell us how it ends. It opens doors, dissolves walls, and shows us options. Shortly after the play begins, we are invited into *How It Ends* and at the end of the play we will be how it ends. A pretty spectacular, profoundly theatrical trick.

Michael Sobota, August 2022

Supposedly retired, Michael Sobota continues his writing career providing critical reviews of books, plays, art, musicians, and cultural organizations. Most recently, he led a workshop on writing literary criticism for the Northwestern Ontario Writers Workshop. He lives in Thunder Bay, Ontario.

How It Ends was first produced by Sick + Twisted Theatre as part of Prairie Theatre Exchange's Leap Series in Winnipeg from April 18–28, 2019, with the following cast and creative team:

Bart: Andrew Cecon
Natalie: Johanna Riley
Sheila: Marie-Josée Chartier
Angel: Debbie Patterson

Directed by Arne MacPherson
Set and Costume Design: Rebekah Enns
Set and Costume Design Assistant: Sean McMullen
Lighting Design: Hugh Conacher
Composition and Sound Design: Dasha Plett
Stage Manager: Katherine Johnston
Production Manager: Brooklyne Alexander

PTE Production Team

Production Manager: Wayne Buss
Technical Director: Sean Neville
Head of Wardrobe: Brenda McLean
Props Master: Elana Honcharuk
Head of Lights and Sound: Cari Simpson
Head Carpenter: Steven Vande Vyvere

Characters

NATALIE: Sister of Bart, daughter of Sheila. Natalie is a palliative care nurse.

BART: Brother of Natalie, son of Sheila. Bart is a minister.

THE ANGEL: The Angel is our guide in all the metaphysical places we visit. They are a wheelchair user or somehow visibly disabled. This character must be played by an actor with a disability.

SHEILA: Having died before the play begins, Sheila exists only in the metaphysical places.

Setting

Scene One: The Boat is set about thirty years into the future. The boat is a classic rowboat floating in a classic lake, in the classic Canadian wilderness. It is performed in a perfect proscenium setting.

Scene Two: The Journey is in a world without time. The journey promenades the audience through a tunnel of sorts that feels very close and contained. Sound and lighting should be used to create a magical atmosphere that is dark and mysterious without being threatening.

Scene Three: The Cloud is also in a world without time. The space feels bright and expansive. The audience sits in a circle facing inward.

Scene Four: The Wake is a church basement or visitation room in a funeral home in present day. This scene should take place in the same location as Scene One, but the space must be reconfigured to be unrecognizable to the audience. The seats they were in in the first scene are hidden from view in this scene, revealed only for the curtain call.

Scene One: The Boat

BART and NATALIE are fishing in a little boat. The light bounces off the water, tiny waves lap against the boat. NATALIE sticks a worm on her hook.

NATALIE: Hold still, little fellow.

BART: It hardly seems fair. Kill the worm to feed the fish. Kill the fish to feed yourself.

NATALIE: The worm gets its revenge, in the end.

BART: "A man may fish with the worm that hath eat of a king. And eat of the fish that hath fed of that worm."

TOGETHER: *Hamlet.*

NATALIE: "They give birth astride of a grave, the light gleams an instant, then it's night once more."

BART: Samuel Beckett?

NATALIE: Yup.

BART: "We are all on death row."

Beat, NATALIE *doesn't know.*

No?

NATALIE: No. Who?

BART: I'm shocked.

NATALIE still doesn't know.

No? You're going to kick yourself.

NATALIE: Mom?

BART: Good guess, but no.

NATALIE: Who?

BART: Elisabeth Kübler-Ross.

NATALIE: Uggghhhh, of course.

BART: And that's Bart one, Natalie zero.

NATALIE: It's not her best one-liner.

BART: First time I heard it, I remember thinking, "Oooh what an amazingly difficult truth that is." And it took me a long time to decide that it isn't true at all, at least in my opinion. It was a really glib thing to say. "We are all on death row," as if the circumstances of your life are irrelevant, it's just senseless.

NATALIE: Agreed.

BART: And I'm not going to walk into your hospice where some poor soul is struggling for breath, take their hand, look them in the eye and say, "I know, me too."

NATALIE: Go ahead, I'm not there anymore.

BART: You're not there yet.

NATALIE: We'll both be there soon enough. Oh, here's one: "The trouble is, you think you have time."

BART: Not a clue.

NATALIE: Ha! Jack Kornfield. Tie game.

BART: No way. I should've got that one.

NATALIE: It has been the map for how I spend the rest of my life, until I don't have any life anymore.

BART: Hovering between retirement and death.

NATALIE: No one gets out of here alive. "The trouble is, you think you have time." Do whatever you do now, pay attention to it, get on with it, and don't think about ten years from now.

BART: You probably don't have ten years.

NATALIE: Precisely.

BART: Okay, but then there's the, the um, whose fallacy is it?

NATALIE: Whose fallacy is what?

BART: The one that says infinite—infinity is never reachable. I'm seventy-three years old—I know that the vast majority of my life is over. But I still don't know when the end is coming and in that sense there is still, there's still . . . an infinite amount of time left.

NATALIE: And even more infinity in the great beyond.

BART: Infinity plus infinity?

NATALIE: Inconceivable.

> *BART rows for a few strokes, whistling "Row, Row, Row Your Boat." He lets the boat coast gently.*

BART: I'm feeling very fit right now. But I look at these old people on the street shuffling along and I'm like, "You poor old fucker." But that's coming down the pike right away whether I like it or not. And I really don't want to think about it.

NATALIE: You don't have to go through it. Mom didn't.

BART: True.

NATALIE: Besides, you might stay hale and hearty as your mind turns to mush.

BART: Yeah, what's going to give out on me first, my mind or my body? If my body goes that's going to be horrible, and if my mind goes that's going to be horrible in a different way.

NATALIE: If you could choose, which would it be: your mind or your body?

BART: Oh God, I don't like this game. If I had to choose, I would probably pick that my body would go. But that would be a drag. A downhill road to not being able to do the things I love anymore. Loss after loss after loss and then dying.

NATALIE: But if your mind went . . . ignorance is bliss.

BART: Thomas Gray.

NATALIE: Really! I would've guessed Shakespeare.

BART: Nope. Thomas Gray.

NATALIE: Go figure.

BART: Something that I have grappled with but have not wrestled into submission yet is the question of—how silly is this going to sound—the way we die, how you die. With nobility, with strength and courage, with bravery with . . . you know? Or a kind of whimpering, frightened, peeing-your-pants ridiculousness. There is something about dying a noble death which I kind of aspire to, you know?

NATALIE: Okay, that is definitely Shakespeare. "Nothing in his life became him like the leaving it. He died as one that studied—

BART and NATALIE talk over each other for the next four lines. It is slightly competitive.

BART: HAD // been studied—

NATALIE: Had been // studied in his death to throw away the dearest thing he owed as if t'were—

BART: *(racing to say it first)* —in his death to throw away the dearest thing he owed as if t'were a trifle."

NATALIE: —a CARELESS trifle."

BART: Damn! I don't even know what it is. I just know that I still have this unresolved issue with hoping that I have a kind of a noble end.

Pause. They both give their attention to their fishing rods.

I spent a lot of time with people who were dying. Not as much as you of course, but during my chaplaincy. I mean it's no secret that the, um—the attrition rate at most churches is dangerously high. I put in a lot of bedside hours. So, I'm not afraid of death, per se. I'm not afraid of being dead and what—

NATALIE: "What dreams may come?"

BART: "What dreams may come," exactly. That doesn't worry me at all. I'm a little bit uncomfortable, I am a little afraid of dying.

NATALIE: What, the pain? Because we can medicate . . .

BART: I'm not afraid of that, I don't look forward to it, I don't want it.

NATALIE: What's the fear?

BART: I'm actually afraid of being conscious of losing forever the one thing that I still am attached to and that is being conscious. Being aware. Experiencing the darkness. The consciousness slipping away. That, I think, is the best I can say to say what frightens me about it. That will be scary. Being aware. Once it's gone it's gone. But the going scares me.

NATALIE: But why miss it? You're only going to do it once.

BART: Says who?

NATALIE: This body is only going to die once. And when this body dies, I want to be there.

BART: But how? In a panic or out of my mind with misery, that's a hell of a way to go.

NATALIE: You think the way Mom did it was better?

BART: Maybe it was, I'm just—I like having pleasure in my life and if at some point I could no longer have Häagen-Dazs, or really nice red wine . . . I'm not interested in quantity; I don't need to be a hundred and eight. I've had a great ride. Why do I have to hang on for what might happen?

NATALIE: Because it, it would be interesting.

BART: Yeah, yeah, yeah. But what about pleasure?

It begins to rain.

NATALIE: Dammit.

BART: Now they'll start biting.

NATALIE: I can be very interested in things that are not pleasurable. They're just interesting, you know? I want to know, I want to pay attention to that. And it's not because it's giving me great pleasure—

BART: Yes, it does. You, I've seen you. You're a burro. You will pursue that little thing until you get an answer and you take great delight in that. It's one of the things I like about you.

Waves get bigger and begin rocking the boat.

NATALIE: So maybe we're differentiating between physical pleasures and mental or intellectual pleasures, perhaps.

BART: Great conversation. If, if I don't have access to people who are intelligent. If I get surrounded by stupidity and ignorance—

Through the next line the rain builds in intensity.

NATALIE: Do you ever run into people who are clearly intelligent, clearly clever, but at the same time just really stupid? Brilliant people who make patently dangerously ridiculous choices. And yet on the surface of things they appear to be very intelligent people.

BART: I would lay claim to some of those behaviours myself. I think I'm a pretty intelligent person and I claim to some behaviour . . .

NATALIE: Well, me too. Okay, maybe that's what it is. I'm an idiot.

We all do I suppose. I'm just not very tolerant when I see them in other people who—

There is a great crack of thunder and a dazzling flash of lightning. The rain goes silent. The stage is black. The back door of the theatre opens and the ANGEL appears backlit in the doorway. She moves in, lights come up a bit to reveal NATALIE and BART, dressed all in white, standing beside the boat.

ANGEL: How wonderful! You'll find what you're looking for through that door. Just follow the light.

NATALIE and BART exit. The ANGEL turns to the audience.

You must come too.

She might have to convince them. But once they're up, she leads them out.

Scene Two: The Journey

The ANGEL leads the audience through a passageway that leads to the cloud. On the way, we hear this:

ANGEL: In this universe, as far as I know, there's only a little bit of life. And when you look at the planet from the space station, and see that thin layer of atmosphere, and you look beyond it: the black, cold immensity of space.

Yes, there's a billion, billion, billion, billion stars in the galaxy, but there is a big unknown, that we don't really know. We can speculate.

I think it is true that there is life throughout the universe. In fact, I hold with a very old mode of thought that everything is alive. That what is truly real is living consciousness. And that our material world of measurable energy and matter and dimensions is merely a reflection of that greater, truer reality.

The idea of collective consciousness that underlies everything, and our eternal being in it, and all that sort of thing.

And our current manifestation, where we can only be in one place at one time, that sort of thing, that limiting sort of thing is an illusion. So within that paradigm, death is a much less significant phenomena.

I'm a Platonic sort of thinker.

Scientists, physicists, and others, philosophers, they're very caught in the human-centric sense of life. The explanations they offer are so fantastical.

I can't credit them either. They don't inspire any confidence in me. So I hold to my intuitive sense of what reality really is.

Scene Three: The Cloud

One by one the people file into a magical place: a circular room with billowy, translucent walls lined with chairs. They are welcomed in and invited to take a seat. SHEILA dances silently around the people as they find their way to their chairs. Once all have arrived, SHEILA ends her dance and the ANGEL begins.

ANGEL: We find ourselves in a moment of "what if."

What if you went to the theatre and were sitting pleasantly watching a show about a brother and sister fishing on the lake when suddenly their boat was struck by lightning. What if you were led down a hallway into a room and then down another hallway and into another room and now you find yourself in a place that definitely isn't a theatre, unsure of what happens next. Dreading the possibility of audience participation.

Or, what if this place is magic? What if you've come here to be transformed?

What if you went to the theatre and were sitting pleasantly watching a show when suddenly the theatre was struck by lightning. What if a benevolent and charming spirit lead you through a journey to a magical place, a place of transformation, leaving you unsure of what happens next. Dreading the possibility that you may have just died.

It could happen.

How are you feeling about that? Wishing you could have had just a little more time? Most of us, when faced with death, wish we could just have a little more time.

But what if this is it? What if the car swerved at just the right moment? What if you had already been vaccinated against the deadly virus you were exposed to as an infant? What if the pilot managed to land the plane without you ever knowing there was a problem? What if this is the little more time that you wished for? What are you going to do with it?

Well, I know what you're going to do first. You're going to watch a scene where a brother and sister arrive—

> *The ANGEL is cut off by the sounds of distant yelling, getting quickly closer. NATALIE and BART burst into the space. SHEILA, their mother, appears seated in an armchair. NATALIE and BART cross the room and sit at her feet.*

SHEILA: You two were too young when it happened. You wouldn't remember your Aunt Jackie. For me it's unforgettable.

Her cancer metastasized to her spine. Untreatable. She knew. She asked her doctor, "Tell me how I will die," and these are his exact words:

"First your legs will go. Then your arms. Then your hands. At the end you will be completely paralyzed. The last thing to go will be the breathing mechanism, and you will slowly suffocate to death." Look what the medical profession is willing to let us go through.

Look at what society thinks is acceptable. She went from being five foot ten to being shorter than I am. I'm five foot four. She was unrecognizable: big barrel body, little skinny legs, big round face, from the prednisone. And long, fine, dark hairs on her face and on her hands and arms . . . Blemishes. She was . . . I would use the word . . . I could use the word freaky and I wouldn't be lying. One day she said to me, "I need to show you what my body looks like. Are you willing to look at me?" And I said yes. She said, "No one has seen all of me. Naked. Not my husband, not my doctor, no one has seen me the way I am, and I need to share it." So we went up into the bedroom and locked the door and she took off all of her clothes.

And it was unspeakable.

She did everything she could with her clothing to disguise how she looked. There are no words. I could say nothing. And all she could do was stand in front of the mirror. "Oh Jackie." And I wept and wept and wept. And she went like this, "Well. Well. Well."

SHEILA *lightly bounces her fist off her thigh.*

I refuse to suffer like that. I won't make you watch me do it. Suffering is wrong. And there is some suffering only death can end.

BART *approaches with the intent to dispute her claim, but he is interrupted.*

ANGEL: Hey! No one wants to watch other people suffer. And nobody wants to suffer. But some say that all life is suffering. So are we all suffering right now? Is this what suffering feels like? Is suffering the price we pay for staying alive?

SHEILA: If I thought God did this, that this was part of a plan, I'd stand outside a different church every Sunday and I would have a placard that would tell you what I thought of God. Because it's so stupid. It is so naïve.

ANGEL: Okay! If God doesn't want us to suffer, should we all just end it right now? Put ourselves out of our misery? Is that what you mean? Or am I being stupid and naïve?

BART: The Stoics differentiate between pain and suffering. In their belief system, pain is a teacher and suffering is unnecessary. With self-discipline, we can choose whether or not to suffer. We can experience pain, but not let it take over our minds.

ANGEL: Whoa! So we shouldn't end it all. We should just use our self-discipline, our awesome mental powers to override the pain. And then we're not suffering. Right? Does that actually sound doable?

NATALIE: I've been working in palliative care long enough that I've seen remarkable strides in our ability to control pain and suffering in the final stages of life. The drugs now are so good, that nobody needs to suffer. We can support you through that.

ANGEL: Sweet! So we don't have to suffer, and we don't have to die and we don't even have to use our self-discipline. We can just use drugs and numb out. We don't have to feel a thing. Nice.

BART: Different religions or spiritual practices or belief systems address the issue of suffering in different ways. But whether it's fasting, or self-flagellation, or endurance rituals, they all have the same goal of building character through discipline. Suffering in order to achieve a higher state.

ANGEL: Wait. So, no drugs?

SHEILA: The next time you have a root canal, you tell your dentist that you're doing it without freezing, invite your whole family to come around and watch you suffer. I don't know the last time you felt pain, but I know when I have. And it's unspeakable. Pain fills every inch of your brain and helplessness fills it too. If you want to decide for yourself, "I'm becoming a better person because of this," then you go ahead and become a better person. If there's value in suffering, it's as simple as that. I know I'm dying, but I just want to skip the torture part. And get right to the death part.

ANGEL: Okay! This is the crux of the issue. This is where the rubber hits the road. Because the torture part, that she wants to skip, that's actually a chapter in your life. But according to you it's a chapter that's going to suck so why bother.

SHEILA: Right.

SHEILA exits.

ANGEL: But according to buddy over here, that's the chapter where you get to achieve a higher state; you get to become a fully realized human being, right?

BART: That's right. Thanks for listening.

BART exits.

ANGEL: *(to NATALIE)* And you think we should just suck air relentlessly with the aid of pharmaceuticals?

NATALIE: No. That's not what I meant.

ANGEL: But I don't quite get the point of being alive but not being—

NATALIE: Never mind.

NATALIE exits.

ANGEL: Okay fine. So we basically have two choices. We can hope for a quick and painless death, or we can hope for a death that takes a little longer and may involve some suffering, but through that suffering we gain time and possibly wisdom. Which would you rather have? A quick and painless death or a slow and suffering death? All in favour of a quick and painless death raise your hand.

She picks on someone with their hand down.

You want to suffer? Let me make this perfectly clear. There are only two choices. You either have your hand up or you don't. You either want a quick and painless death or a slow and suffering death. Sorry, this is the mandatory audience participation portion of the show. This is not optional: YOU WILL DIE. So let's call the question again: all in favour of a quick and painless death raise your hand.

But wait. Hands down. No one wants to watch you suffer. How do you think your loved ones will feel about this choice? What if you were the loved one? What if the person dying was the person you love most in the world? Would you want them to die fast and painlessly or slowly with suffering? All in favour of the person you love most in the world dying fast raise your hand!

Oh just pick one. It's no big deal. No one's going to hold you to it.

But wait. Hands down. All life is suffering. So if you have a life partner, one of you is probably going to die first, and one of you is going to live on and suffer. So which one of you is going to die and which one of you is going to live and suffer? All in favour of being the one to die raise your hand, if you want to suffer keep your hand down. One, two, three, VOTE!

Okay, okay, okay, keep your hands where they are. Let's do a quick poll.

She goes around the room pointing at each person.

You're going to suffer. And you're going to die. And you're gonna die. And you're going to die. And you're going to suffer. And you're gonna suffer. Suffer, suffer, die, suffer, die, suffer . . . *(etc.)*

She becomes increasingly distressed until naming the suffering and dying becomes unbearable.

Oh God! I hate this game. I don't want any of you to suffer or die. Why can't we just be immortal? I know! Let's play the game called "How to Be Immortal"!

The other performers come running onto the stage. During the following, they take cards from the ANGEL and distribute one card to each audience member.

Ironic coming from someone like me. I know I know, people like me, you know, "The Disabled," we kind of remind other people, by the way we are, of their own mortality and vulnerability. And people don't seem to like that. They want to pretend that they are invulnerable. Sometimes when people see me, they have to question their belief in their own immortality.

But no more! Each of you has, in your hands, a key to immortality. We are going to get all those keys together and live forever!

Are you ready?

The other performers prepare themselves in the centre of the circle.

On your marks, get set, go!

The performers run to audience members, take their cards from them, run to the centre of the circle, hold up the card, and declare what it says then place the card in the centre of the circle. This is what the cards say:

don't smoke

hide the grey

moisturize

stay fit

detoxify

regular colonics

keep up with pop culture

chelation therapy

be sired by a demigod

avoid chemicals

laugh

eat organic

purge

amass wealth

plastic surgery

hot yoga

protect your telomeres from shrinking

meditate

procreate

cryonic suspension

create great art that will endure forever

stay out of the sun

get enough sleep

exercise daily

stay fashion forward

get off the grid

buckle up

wear a helmet

travel at the speed of light

maintain your fire extinguishers in good working order

live in a home with stairs

look both ways before crossing

never swim alone

care for a pet

go paleo

Botox

floss daily

write witty status updates

cultivate optimism

build community

mentor the young

'invent something

practice gratitude

be short

chiropractic adjustments

achieve greatness

avoid stress

conquer civilizations

get blood transfusions from young healthy donors

have sex frequently

upload your consciousness into an avatar

take your vitamins

exist only on the metaphysical plane

At intervals, the ANGEL repeats what the card says and all the others perform that action for a few seconds. At the end of the game, all the performers collapse exhausted on the floor.

The lights go to black and a voice is heard. A magical, glowing orb appears over the prone figures. It swirls and spins as they move with it.

I had a near death experience when I was quite young—what was I? I was probably in my early twenties. I went out on the porch to take a little bit of the breeze and I felt this great rushing wind behind me. And then I, I looked at the street, the buildings, the lights and suddenly it became like a negative image. Kind of reddish, a reddish negative image. So I, I said to myself, "It's like a trip and I better not fight it." So I just went with it, way out of my body. The sense was that I went up. Up and out into space. I mean there's no way for me to defend that sensation. That's not a rational, sort of documentable, measurable kind of thing. But I, I, in some distance I could see these two glowing objects very clear, very beautiful, very colourful, almost pulsating. And there was a sound coming from them too. There were two of them, but they both were made of these beautiful, kind of neon glowing colours. And had this kind of singing sound coming from them. And I was drawn to them, and I could move my, move in what seemed to be space: left, right, up, down; by just wanting to. By motivation, I guess. So I moved toward them. And I remember nestling in, in the arms of one. We were in some kind of communion. It was quite wonderful. And then I felt a pain. I didn't know what it was. But it was as if it were in my body far below. And it was like a string or a . . . like a cord between me and that body down below. A silver cord. I had the sense that, well I could ignore it. But I better not. That's my body calling, it's in trouble. So I went to woooooo woooooo woooooo woooooo down that string, back into my body. Then I kind of opened my eyes and stirred. I was still sitting on my chair on the porch. And uh, but the sound was gone. And I was sweating, really a lot. And I was cold because the breeze was blowing over my face. And in a moment, I was able to turn around and go inside. And there were my friends, still smoking dope. I've always wondered, was that an out of body experience? Or was that a near death? To this day I don't know.

The lights come up on NATALIE.

NATALIE: I love working in palliative care. People come to us with a clean slate. We only know them as they are when they walk in the door. We are there to provide care for them in this stage that, that they're in. So whatever they struggled with in life, it isn't relevant to what we do, really.

No judgment, just treat everyone with loving kindness.

Some people feel very undeserving when you're providing care for them and they apologize or they feel bad about what you need to do with them, for them. But this is what we do.

BART and SHEILA *begin to move.*

Every common nitty-gritty task is part of supporting someone through this end-of-life process and so all of it is valuable. And all of it's important. So helping you with your toileting is as important as administering your pain meds, or keeping you groomed and clean, or giving emotional support, listening, affirming. It's all important. And it's all valuable. And everybody is worthy of that, whatever care that is.

No matter what you've done, no matter what you've achieved or how you've failed, no matter who you've hurt or how much you've loved, we are here to care for you.

SHEILA: I was an independent woman all my life. I raised my children without a partner at a time when that was not at all acceptable. And I did so, if I may be so bold, with elegance and style. My clothes were pressed, my hair was styled, and my face was on whenever I left the house. We were not an "open bathroom door" sort of family. We appreciated the sense of dignity that privacy provides. This was not effortless. I put a great deal of work into maintaining dignity throughout my life and I'll be damned if I'm going to sacrifice that now. If I don't want to be reduced to an animal-like existence, why should I be forced to do so? I'm making a different choice.

BART: I had, a couple of years ago, what was supposed to be routine surgery—and it went south. I ended up on bedrest. Like I could not get out of bed for five days. "Seriously? The bathroom is two steps away, but I've got to use a bedpan? Oh God!" I found that the hardest in the whole, in the whole thing. My intense sense of loss of control in that little escapade. It really surprised me. I thought I was a bigger person. I'm not. It was certainly humbling. And it's given me great respect for people who live with that day in and day out. Accepting that care with grace: that's hard-core dignity.

The ANGEL appears with a box of shredded toilet paper on her lap. As she speaks, she tosses toilet paper into the air, festooning the audience.

ANGEL: Dignity! Dignity! We all want dignity! Here's some dignity for you. And some dignity for you. And more tattered shreds of dignity for you! *(etc.)*

People talk endlessly about dignity, but when they use that word, we know what they're really saying: "I don't want anyone wiping my ass."

"I'd rather die!"

How much time do you spend each day wiping your butt? Have

you ever timed yourself? Does anyone know, to the second, how long it takes them to wipe their own ass?

Well then let's find out. Let's play a game called "Wipe Your Butt." Just grab a little shred of dignity and then fold, wrap, or scrunch, as you do. And once you're ready we'll start the clock. Ready?

On your marks, get set, wipe your butt! *(starts counting)* One motorboat, two motorboat, three motorboat . . . *(etc.)*

If no one will wipe their butt add this text:

Come on, wipe your butts!

I can't believe you are so reluctant to wipe your butts. Isn't that a valuable part of your day, an activity that you particularly enjoy?

The ANGEL will try to get someone else to wipe their butt as she times them by counting motorboats. If this doesn't work, the ANGEL will wipe her own butt, counting out the motorboats as she does.

One motorboat, two motorboat, three motorboat, four motorboats. And then you check. Oh, I have to go again. Five motorboats, six motorboats, seven motorboats, and then you check again. One more and I should be good. Eight motorboats, nine motorboats, ten motorboats, eleven motorboats. And I'm done! Eleven seconds. It only takes eleven seconds to wipe your butt.

But wait. You might do your number two more than once in a day. If you go twice that's twenty-two seconds, three times that's thirty-three seconds, four times at forty-four seconds, five times—wait.

Nobody does number two more than four times a day. Not on average. So maximum forty-four seconds.

But wait. If you're the kind of person who sits down to pee, you're going to have to wipe then, too. How long does it take you wipe the front bum?

She seeks input from the audience. If she doesn't get it, she just makes it up.

Maybe . . . seven seconds? Okay. So, in that case you would have eleven seconds for your first number two, twenty-two seconds for your second number two, then twenty-nine, thirty-six, forty-three, fifty, fifty-seven, sixty-four, seventy-one. Just a little over a minute. For the whole day.

But wait, I know what you're thinking! Every now and then it's going to take a little longer, right? When it's that time of the month. How much time does it take then?

Again, she seeks input from the audience. If she doesn't get it, she just makes it up.

Should we say maybe thirteen seconds? Okay. So, we have eleven seconds for your first number two, twenty-two seconds for your second number two, and then thirty-five, forty-eight, sixty-one, seventy-four, eighty-seven, a hundred, a hundred and thirteen. Under two minutes. Worst case scenario: you will need two minutes of your day dedicated to butt wiping.

SHEILA enters and begins cleaning up the toilet paper.

I spend two minutes a day doing many things I enjoy. I probably spend two minutes a day laughing. I probably spend two minutes a day reading. I probably spend two minutes a day learning something new. I spend two minutes a day eating something delicious, talking to strangers, cuddling with my sweetheart, there are many things I spend two minutes a day doing that I really enjoy.

But if I can't spend two minutes a day wiping my butt, I'm going to give up on all those other two minuteses. That two minutes of my day is so important that I'm going to call it quits when I can't have that two precious minutes to experience the joy of wiping my own ass.

Man, people must really love wiping their butts. It must be the highlight of their day.

The ANGEL exits. Through the speech, SHEILA continues to clean up all the shreds of toilet paper left behind. She arranges eight rolls of toilet paper in a perfect square and stands in the centre.

SHEILA: In any other context, being forced to allow some stranger to remove your clothing and touch your privates would be illegal. If someone doesn't care, if they're perfectly happy to let anyone into their pants, well then that's fine, that's their business. But that's not me, I don't want to be touched in that way. And if I do not consent, how is that any different from being assaulted? And if I am traumatized by a stranger touching me in an extremely intimate way, that's not me being a prude, that's me being a self-respecting human being. I have boundaries, I don't have to justify them. I wouldn't be called upon to justify my boundaries in any other circumstance. It is unreasonable to subject a person to this kind of assault several times a day, every day for the rest of their life. For me, being forced into that situation, would be nothing short of torture. I value my autonomy and my privacy. I will not be shamed into giving them up. And if I have to sacrifice a couple of weeks of my life in order to maintain my dignity, then it's the price I have to pay. I value my dignity. It is an integral part of who I am.

The ANGEL enters.

ANGEL: I am what I am what I am what I am. How much do you need to be in control in order to feel like you are who you are? What makes you you?

> *BART and NATALIE enter. They each take a roll of toilet paper from SHEILA's carefully constructed square. They each hand the end of the role of toilet paper to an audience member and then walk across the circle draping the toilet paper over SHEILA as they cross and handing the other end to another audience member. Through the following, they create a sort of toilet paper pinwheel with SHEILA at the centre. Meanwhile the ANGEL goes up to individual audience members and asks them these questions:*

What if you had to change your name: would you still be you?

What if you had to wear a uniform all the time: would you still be you?

What if you had to move to a foreign country where you didn't know anyone and you couldn't speak the language: would you still be you?

What if you lost everything you own: would you still be you?

What if you could no longer do your job: would you still be you?

What if you had to spend forty hours a week doing something pointless: would you still be you?

What if you couldn't have sex anymore: would you still be you?

What if you couldn't walk: (that's awkward!) would you still be you?

What if you got a face transplant: would you still be you?

What if you couldn't make things anymore: would you still be you?

What if you couldn't sing or dance anymore: would you still be you?

What if you couldn't remember anything: would you still be you?

What if you were unable to learn new things: would you still be you?

What if you couldn't form complete thoughts anymore: would you still be you?

What if you were shunned by your community: would you still be you?

What if you could no longer express yourself: would you still be you?

What if you couldn't leave the house anymore: would you still be you?

What if you were completely paralyzed: would you still be you?

What if you were in a coma: would you still be you?

WHAT IF YOU WERE IN A COMA: WOULD YOU STILL BE YOU?

The ANGEL exits.

SHEILA: You make it so complicated, but it's not. It's so simple. Life is really so simple.

When I was diagnosed, I had two thoughts. One is, my first thought was, "I lived to raise my children," and I just felt peace. And my second thought was Dignitas. I'm telling you now. I'm going. I'm worthy. And I know that it costs, and it can bankrupt the family, it's eleven thousand dollars just for the procedure. Not counting flying there. Not counting the hotel that you stay in. Not counting bringing family with you. So, you're looking at twenty to thirty thousand dollars. And pah, the inheritance is gone but I get what I want. I told my children, "If I go to Dignitas, you come with me." And my eldest son said, "I could never do it, Mom, I could never . . ." He was crying, "I could never do it." And I said, "Well you know it's a holiday after. And it's what I want."

> *NATALIE and BART approach the audience members who are still holding the ends of the toilet paper. They take the paper and place it on the floor, arranging them so they drape beautifully.*

BART: So, we arrived on a Sunday.

NATALIE: We had to be in Switzerland, um, three days—

BART: Nearly four days before the actual date.

NATALIE: And we all knew what was going to happen on this date. Well for, for us it was very difficult to have, you know, the calendar get closer and closer to that point, but it didn't seem to—

BART: Mom never wavered.

NATALIE: Not for a second.

BART: And, and there were moments where it just felt like a fun family vacation. You know? Well not fun but, but— It was, it was just bizarre. I don't know, I mean it was very gentle and very pleasant and surreal.

NATALIE: It was what she wanted. I think if she had had any choice in life, that would have been it. To be in control. And for everything to be quick and easy, um, and not to bother to anyone.

BART: You know she likes that control.

NATALIE: She had made the decision and it was almost like a disconnect from everything else. The focus was so strong, leading us all to that one thing.

SHEILA begins to turn so the paper wraps around her like a maypole.

SHEILA: I have my pictures ready for the funeral. I'm gonna blow them up, make it easy for the family. I'm going to write my own obituary because I know what I want to say.

And I know exactly how . . . it's all in my mind, it's all planned out and it's going to be, it's going to be just the way—I hope—that it will be just as I wish. Just as I wish.

> NATALIE *and* BART *gather up the ends of the toilet paper and begin wrapping* SHEILA *into a toilet paper shroud. Once the ends are wrapped around her, they each pick up another toilet paper roll and begin walking around her to wrap her up.*

BART: It was outside of Zürich.

NATALIE: They had two staff who were there to meet us.

BART: They were both lovely.

NATALIE: It's set up so that you can have quite a few people attending if you choose. And I think almost virtually everyone chooses to, to remain in one of the rooms that they have, but Mom chose to sit out in the garden.

BART: Because it'd been a really cold winter at home.

NATALIE: Things weren't in full bloom they were just beginning—

BART: No, but it was warm. It was pleasant.

NATALIE: The medication is actually taken in two stages. You have to take a drink that settles your stomach first and you have to wait thirty minutes which um allows this medication to work.

BART: And if you decide you want to wait three hours then they just they just re-administer that one again so there's no pressure, "Oh I've taken this one now I have to—"

NATALIE: Absolutely, you have that whole day, or you can go home. But she—she didn't want to.

BART: No, she was pretty much . . . We—she had a few little "things" she wanted to wrap up.

NATALIE: *(laughing)*

BART: That was another surreal moment. She had some idea—

NATALIE: *(laughing harder)*

BART: —that she wanted to write a few sentences about each grandchild *(breaking up, too)* but she'd gotten busy the night before—

NATALIE: And Bart—

BART: —writing her own obituary.

NATALIE: And Bart was— *(laughing too hard to finish)*

BART: Mom was a very, uh, direct person. And sometimes she wasn't very diplomatic. So she'd write something about her grandchild and then she'd say, "Is that okay?" And I'd say, "No! You can't say that!"

NATALIE: *(hooting with laughter)*

BART: You can't say that. And so she'd say, "Well, what should I, how should I say it?" So I said, "Well why don't you say it like this."

NATALIE: Our brother has three children.

BART: Three?

NATALIE: And he says to our mother, "Well, what about Vladislav?" And I said to her, "Who is Vladislav?"

BART: *(laughing)*

NATALIE: He had a fourth child. That she'd never told us about.

BART: That had happened a couple of years earlier. So we're all sitting around and then there's, "What about Vladislav?" And um, and there's just this silence.

NATALIE: Well because our brother was there with his wife, who—

BART: With his wife who is not Vladislav's mother.

NATALIE: Yes yes yes.

BART: So then in this awkward silence, you piped up, "Well! Is there anything else that anyone would like to share?"

NATALIE: *(uproarious laughter)*

BART: So that was that.

Beat.

And then she asked for the drink.

SHEILA: I know exactly what I want. I know exactly. I want all my family, nieces, nephew, brother-in-law, and his new wife. I want everyone there. I want private time with my children. Then I want my sister and my nieces and nephew. I want Kathleen Battle. Right? Is that the opera singer? Singing, "Over My Head, I Hear Music In The Air, There Must Be A God Somewhere." I want her voice singing that. And then I want to swallow what I need to swallow, and I want it done. Simple as that.

Let's face it, this life isn't all that great. We're not going to get out of it alive so why would I worry.

NATALIE: It's, it's, it's very bitter.

BART: The drink is very bitter so they take—and so she took a piece of chocolate

NATALIE: Yes, they give you chocolate.

BART: She was, she was incredible, right to the last actually. Eating her chocolates and wearing, she was wearing this little paper crown that one of the grandkids made, I think. And in her nightie she had this lovely, she had party dresses, you don't mind me telling . . .

NATALIE: No no.

BART: She loved all her dresses so she started wearing them a lot more. And she was wearing a very nice dress the day we went to, um, Dignitas. But she brought along this nightie and she went and changed into this nightie that had some funny cartoon on it. I still remember. So there she was and the man from Dignitas was so sweet he said, "Sheila," he said, "That was such a pretty dress." He said, he said, "You don't, you didn't have to change into that nightie. We would've looked after the dress." And Mom said, "But I always have such a good sleep in this." And she just smiled. Yeah, it was, she was actually quite charming.

NATALIE: Yeah—

BART: And, and then she said, "Well, maybe we should sing something."

NATALIE: We are very much a non-musical family.

BART: We're not only non-musical, we are a very reserved family. So I, I said, I was trying to think of something everyone knew, so I said, "What about "Row, Row, Row Your Boat"? We can do it in a round." I was just kind of joking. So we started doing "Row, Row, Row Your Boat" in a round and she was singing.

NATALIE: It's, it's extremely gentle, in that it's, it's literally falling asleep and it takes two minutes. It's just two minutes.

SHEILA is shrouded in toilet paper now, only her face is uncovered.

BART: Yeah, and then she stopped singing.

SHEILA begins singing "Over My Head." As she sings, BART wraps her head in toilet paper. Once she's completely wrapped, the singing stops and BART and NATALIE lay her down on the floor. BART stays with her, and NATALIE cleans up.

NATALIE: I, I, I don't revisit it a lot in my mind.

BART: No.

NATALIE: She made a choice. Um, and a choice that didn't surprise anyone who knew her well. And she, she walked to it without any, I don't think she even had any regrets. I, I can't say that she did.

BART: I think what she was able to do, was to look, look ahead as opposed to "what if" and—

NATALIE: No looking back.

BART: She just didn't do that, she just kept looking forward. Um—

NATALIE: You were caught up. We, we all were just followers, I think. We had to leave everything aside and just follow her lead.

BART: So then after, when Mom was no longer . . . in charge, we all sort of drifted—

NATALIE: I think it is easier to be the one who dies than one who survives and, and you don't want to say those things out loud always, but it's the truth.

BART: Oh absolutely.

NATALIE: It's the truth. It's never just about the person ever. It can't be.

There's nothing simple about that choice. Nothing. Nothing easy about that choice because it involves so many people who will struggle with it on various levels. I would never have tried to physically stop her. I don't think we have the right to say "you can't do that" for us. Because that, too is selfish. Where do you find that perfect balance that meets the needs of everyone: the person who is making that choice and the people who want to care for them.

In practice I don't think it happens in the way that people want it to. Things never do. They never can. It took a tremendous amount of courage in many ways, in many ways. Setting a date and walking toward it without, without wavering at any point or in any way. It takes incredible courage. But there's also a little bit of weakness. This idea that you can't allow things to, you know, be taken out of your control. So it's, it's not straightforward.

> *BART crosses to NATALIE, takes her hand, and leads her out the door, leaving SHEILA, still shrouded, on the floor. ANGEL enters.*

ANGEL: Death is big, death is messy. Your children will not be able to wad it up in a tissue and tuck it up their sleeves, no matter how neat and tidy you try to make it. And though thousands and thousands of people die every day and yours will be one tiny drop in a sea of mortality, your death will change the shape of the world around you.

But what if? What if the line between life and death isn't as sudden as we think? What if we can hover in the space between for a while?

Without a constant supply of blood, our cells will begin to die, but not all at once. The cells in our brains will live for three to seven minutes after we are actually dead. The cells in our skin and our bones will survive the longest, lasting several days. How remarkable that our bodies continue to live after our hearts stop beating. And if the body is still living, it's hard to imagine that the soul would fly off all at once at the moment of death. Maybe it will gently peel away as the living cells in our perfect, beautiful bodies, one by one, slowly succumb to starvation? Will we be aware of the process? Will the living cells of the skin know when they're being touched several days after death?

But we are more than our bodies, so how do we define the other parts of who we are? Our souls? Our minds? Our personalities?

If all of these things are immaterial objects, can they be destroyed by death which is a material process? Or maybe the mistake is in thinking of them as objects: as nouns and not verbs. What if the soul is an action?

We so value being in control of everything, but death defies our mastery. We can't control it. And if we're lucky, once we realize that, we finally figure it out.

We are not in control. We never were. We are in a place of magic. We have come here to be transformed. Surrender to the chaos. Step into the unknown. Embrace the mystery.

Because what comes next is a big surprise!

> *Suddenly balloons fall from the ceiling, music plays. The ANGEL and SHEILA dance and play with the balloons. The ANGEL invites members of the audience to join them. NATALIE and BART appear in the doorway, dressed in funeral attire.*

BART: Excuse me everyone. We are ready for you.

NATALIE: If you would just come this way, please.

> *BART and NATALIE lead the audience out of the circular place, through a passageway, and into the final destination.*

Scene Four: The Wake

*The audience is led from the circle through a hallway into a
room that looks like a funeral home. They file past NATALIE and
BART, in a receiving line, followed by a casket opened to reveal
a mirror where the face should be. On the other side of the room
is a table with a guestbook, a plate of cookies, and an urn of
coffee. The audience stands for this scene. There is a church pew
for those who need to sit.*

Once everyone has arrived, they begin the eulogy.

BART: Thank you all for coming. It means a lot to us.

NATALIE: If you will just humour us for a few more minutes, we each
have a story about Mom that we would like to share. Bart, would
you go first?

BART: I think you should go first.

NATALIE: Mmm, I thought we agreed—

BART: That's not— Okay, I'll start first.

When Mom had got the final diagnosis, she contacted all of her
friends. She had dozens and dozens of friends.

Now you start.

NATALIE: Umm. Okay. When I got my first job, Mom tried to instill in me an understanding of the "value of a dollar." She made me do the math to figure out how much I was really paid for every hour I gave to my job. You go.

BART: As people came to visit her, she would recount to them all her memories of their friendship, beginning with how they met.

NATALIE: I had to add prep and travel time to the hours I worked. Then I had to subtract the money I spent on work: bus fare, work clothes from my take-home pay. And then I could see how much I was actually getting paid—how much one hour of my life was worth.

BART: So if you'd come to see her she would say "_____ *(names someone in the room)*, we met in 1962 at Normal School and remember when we did XYZ and thus and so."

NATALIE: When we would go shopping, she would convert all the prices into hours of my life and then ask me, "Are those shoes really worth it? Are you willing to give up a week of your life to have those shoes sitting in your closet?"

BART: And then she would describe to them how that friendship had impacted her life. She would say, "The things that I really treasure about our friendship are:" and she kind of named them.

NATALIE: I have never been able to shop without thinking about how much of my life I'm giving up to have the things I'm buying. Two days ago, I was at the grocery store and I could hear Mom's voice in my ear, "Forty-five minutes of your life for a pineapple? Will you really enjoy it that much?"

BART: And Mom was pretty blunt, so sometimes she'd say things that maybe she could've kept to herself. But still, it was specific and personal from the heart so you couldn't take offence. Or maybe she just knew no one would call her on it, she could get away with it. She was dying, so . . .

NATALIE: I was standing there holding the pineapple and I had this vision of all the people who had touched that pineapple before me: the farmer, the harvester, the kid who put it on the display shelf, all of them had put their lives into bringing this pineapple to me. To feed me. The pineapple I was holding contained a little life from each of these people.

BART: It was just such an honouring, such a generous recognition of how their lives had impacted hers, how the gift of their time, their friendship had enriched her life.

NATALIE: My life was being sustained by theirs. And by paying for it, hopefully, their lives were being sustained by mine.

BART: We all rely so much on each other, but we forget. We forget to notice, we forget to acknowledge, we forget to express gratitude. But, at the end of every visit, after recounting the special connection she had shared with the person, she'd say, "So thank you for being my friend."

NATALIE: So I give this to you as a way to remember my mom. To remember that our lives are sustained by the work of strangers, and that our actions and choices in turn sustain the lives of people we will never meet. We are all connected.

And it's okay to cry in the produce department from time to time.

BART: All life on this earth is sustained by the death of other things. So, what life will be sustained by your death? What is waiting for you to die in order to grow? And if you could, where would you choose to transfer the energy that is you after your death? How will you make your death as life-giving as it possibly can be?

NATALIE: So, I want to say thank you. Thank you for sharing your lives with me, to nourish my body.

BART: And in that spirit, I want to thank all the people here.

NATALIE: And all the people not here.

BART: All the people that have come before.

NATALIE: And all those yet to come.

BART: We are all in this together.

NATALIE: We are all connected. Please stay as long as you like.

The walls open to reveal the ANGEL and SHEILA sitting in the audience seats from the first scene. BART and NATALIE join them and they applaud the audience, who now find themselves on stage.

The End

Acknowledgements

Many people participated in the development of this script: some as artists who workshopped the play with me and some as interview subjects whose words are included in this text. I'd like to offer my deepest, most heartfelt thanks to all of them: Heidi Taylor, Arne MacPherson, Eric Blais, Johanna Riley, Gislina Patterson, Aurora Thiessen, Sara Constable, Andrew Cecon, Pedro Chamale, Stephen Hill, Sylvi MacCormac, Lisa Cooke Ravensbergen, Jeff MacKay, Michael Sobota, Sheila Dunn Noyes, Cindy Rublee, Natasha, barb janes, Rose Marie Reimer, Ian Scott, Jim Derksen, Lisa Shaw, and Mabel Shaw.

I also wish to express deepest gratitude to Solmund MacPherson, Orion Smith, Robert Metcalfe, Thomas Morgan Jones, the staff of Prairie Theatre Exchange, my fellow playwrights from the PTE Playwrights Unit: Joseph Aragon, Sharon Bajer, Rick Chafe, Ginny Collins, Trish Cooper, James Durham, Ellen Peterson, Ian Ross, and my fellow playwrights from the Playwrights Theatre Centre Colony: Peter Anderson, Sunny Drake, and José Teodoro.

The development of this play was supported by the Manitoba Arts Council and the Canada Council for the Arts.

Writing this play was informed by many experiences in my life, but the two most notable are:

1. The astonishing work done by Lillian Vilborg MacPherson and her beloveds as she prepared to die.

2. The tiny, ever-growing scars in my brain that teach me how to be human.

Finally, forever and always love unbounded to my most wonderful Arne MacPherson.

Debbie Patterson is a Winnipeg playwright, director, and actor. Trained at the National Theatre School of Canada, she is a founding member of Shakespeare in the Ruins (SIR), and the founder and current artistic director of Sick + Twisted Theatre. Playwriting credits include *How It Ends*, *Sargent & Victor & Me* (both for Sick + Twisted Theatre), the musicals *Head* (SIR) and *Molotov Circus* (SummerWorks), and numerous TYA shows for Prairie Theatre Exchange. In 2016, Debbie became the first physically disabled actor to play the title role in *Richard III* in a professional Canadian production. She was honoured with the United Nations Platform for Action Committee Manitoba's 2014 Activist Award and the 2017 Winnipeg Arts Council Making a Mark Award. She was twice shortlisted for the Gina Wilkinson Prize. She is the matriarch of a family of artists and a proud advocate for disability justice, living a wheelchair-enabled life in Winnipeg and in a cabin on the shore of Lake Winnipeg with her partner and collaborator, Arne MacPherson.